INVESTIGATING THE UNEXPLAINED

GHOSTS

By Emily Rose Oachs

BELLWETHER MEDIA • MINNEAPOLIS, MN

Blastoff! Discovery launches
a new mission: reading to learn.
Filled with facts and features, each
book offers you an exciting new
world to explore!

This edition first published in 2019 by Bellwether Media, Inc.

Library of Congress Cataloging-in-Publication Data

Names: Oachs, Emily Rose, author.
Title: Ghosts / by Emily Rose Oachs.
Description: Minneapolis, MN : Bellwether Media, Inc., 2019.
  Series: Blastoff! Discovery: Investigating the Unexplained
  Includes bibliographical references and index.
Identifiers: LCCN 2018003674 (print) | LCCN 2018008767
  (ebook) | ISBN 9781626178533 (hardcover : alk. paper)
  ISBN 9781681035949 (ebook)
Subjects: LCSH: Ghosts–Juvenile literature. | Parapsychology–
  Juvenile literature.
Classification: LCC BF1461 (ebook) | LCC BF1461 .O185 2019
  (print) | DDC 133.1–dc23

LC record available at https://lccn.loc.gov/2018003674

Editor: Paige Polinsky   Designer: Andrea Schneider

Printed in the United States of America, North Mankato, MN.

TABLE OF CONTENTS

WHAT WAS THAT?

An old man leads Sasha and Otto to the front door of an empty prison. A giant ring of keys jangles in his hands. "I don't go in after dark," he says gruffly. "That's when the ghosts cause trouble." Sasha and Otto grin. Ghosts are what they hope to find.

The man pushes the creaky door open. Sasha and Otto step inside. Paint peels from the walls, and dust covers the floor. Otto aims his flashlight. It lights a path deeper into the old prison.

REC

5

The **investigators** stop in a hallway lined with prison cells. Otto fills his notepad. He tracks the date, time, and temperature. Sasha waves a small device around the room. Then Sasha and Otto both hear something. Footsteps. But they are alone in the prison!

Suddenly, a cell door clangs shut behind them.
Sasha spins toward the door. Her device beeps, and
its lights begin to flash. It is picking up on something
close! Is there a ghost nearby?

MYSTERIOUS SPIRITS

Many people believe ghosts are the **souls** of people who have died. These souls remain among the living instead of moving to the **afterlife**. Hauntings are often reported at places that have seen disasters. Some ghosts are said to cause trouble. Others communicate more peacefully.

Flickering lights and strange noises may mean a ghost is present. Shadows or strange figures may also appear. There are even reports of ghosts pushing people or pulling their hair!

LEFT BEHIND

Believers think that some souls become ghosts because they died suddenly. Others might become ghosts because they left something undone.

THE HUNT BEGINS

For thousands of years, ghosts have appeared in stories worldwide. In the United States, modern ghost hunting began in 1848. Sisters Kate and Maggie Fox were **mediums**. They claimed ghosts communicated with them through tapping sounds. Their work helped inspire a religion called **Spiritualism**.

Kate and Maggie Fox

séance

WHITE HOUSE SPIRITS

In 1862, President Abraham Lincoln's young son, Willie, died. First Lady Mary Todd hoped to get in touch with Willie through a medium. She hosted several séances in the White House.

séance

Spiritualists tried to contact ghosts through **séances**. During séances, people held hands in a circle. A medium then connected them with the dead. Some mediums claimed spirits spoke through them! Séances were popular around the **Civil War**. People hoped to speak with loved ones lost in battle.

spirit photo, 1800s

spirit photo, 1800s

New discoveries gave ghost hunters fresh investigation methods. In 1861, a photo showing a shadowy "ghost" made photography a key tool. People began taking hundreds of spirit photos. Many were determined fake by groups like the Society for **Psychical** Research. British scientists founded this society in 1882 to study **paranormal** activity.

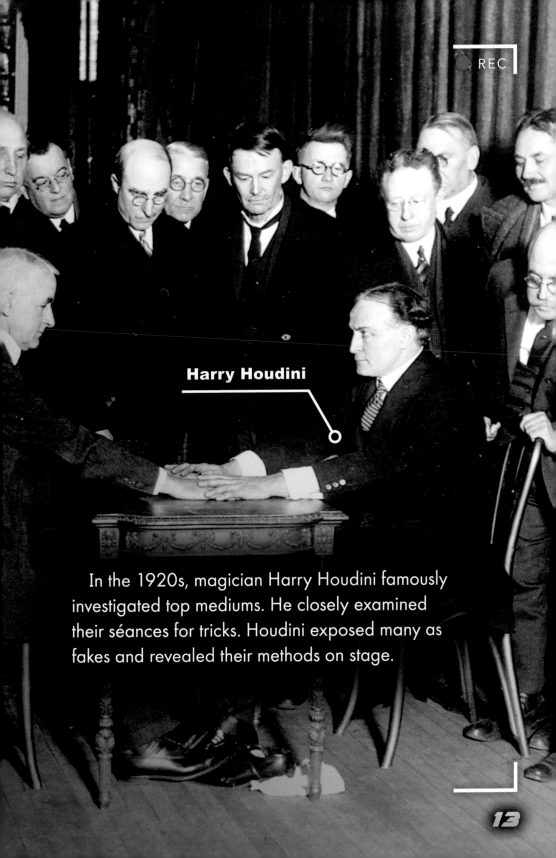

Harry Houdini

In the 1920s, magician Harry Houdini famously investigated top mediums. He closely examined their séances for tricks. Houdini exposed many as fakes and revealed their methods on stage.

WHO YA GONNA CALL?

In the 1920s, inventor Thomas Edison
wanted to build a "spirit phone."
He hoped it would allow people to
speak directly with the dead!

investigator on
Ghost Hunters TV show

The 1930s brought early recordings of spirit voices. In 1959, artist Friedrich Jurgenson explored **audio recordings** further. The **electronic voice phenomena** (EVP) gave investigators a new type of **evidence**!

By the 1980s, ghost hunting had moved from the séance table to the big screen. The 1984 film *Ghostbusters* brought ghost hunting to the public's attention. In the 1990s, new paranormal television shows aired. These programs presented the most advanced gear. They pulled modern ghost hunting into the **mainstream**.

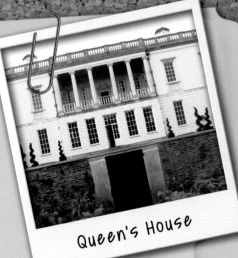
Queen's House

PROFILE: THE TULIP STAIRCASE PHOTOGRAPH

In 1966, Reverend Ralph Hardy visited the Queen's House in Greenwich, England. He took many photos. After developing them, Hardy saw a ghostly figure on the Tulip Staircase. Experts studied the photo but found no trickery.

In 1967, paranormal investigator Peter Underwood visited the house. His team sealed it off to outsiders. They examined the staircase and held a séance. Some heard odd sounds, and an audio recorder captured a baby crying. But cameras and thermometers found no evidence. The mystery of the Tulip Staircase photo remains unsolved.

Peter Underwood

ghostly figure on the Tulip Staircase

BORLEY RECTORY

Peter Underwood also studied hauntings at Borley Rectory. This home was the site of ghostly activities for many years. It was known as the most haunted house in England!

GOING ON A GHOST HUNT

Ghost hunters today fill their tool kits with the latest technology. Many use devices that track an area's **electromagnetic field** (EMF). Investigators believe the EMF changes when a ghost is present. EMF meters track the levels in a room.

HOW EMF METERS WORK

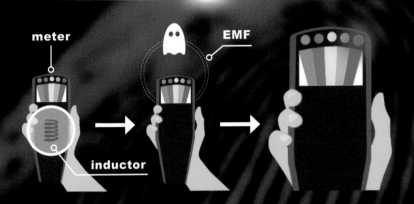

meter

EMF

inductor

1. The meter contains a small wire coil. This is called an inductor.

2. When the meter passes through an EMF, the inductor creates a tiny flow of electricity.

3. A device called an amplifier makes this flow stronger.

4. The electricity is measured, and a light turns on to display the results.

Not all tools need to be high-tech. A simple notebook, pencil, and flashlight are useful in any investigation. Some investigators carry objects that were connected to the person in life. These items are meant to attract the ghost.

audio recorder

Audio recorders help ghost hunters capture EVP. Often, hunters record themselves asking questions to an empty room. They pause after each question. The investigators may not hear anything unusual during this process. But later, the recording may reveal mysterious EVP between their questions.

INVESTIGATOR TOOLBOX

EMF meter

audio recorder

thermal camera

ambient thermometer

video camera

Some investigators use spirit boxes to hear ghosts. These devices scan through radio stations. Ghosts might piece the **static** and sound clips together to form words. Some people believe static may give ghosts the energy they need to communicate.

orb

Cameras are key for gathering proof of ghosts.
Photographs may show balls of light called orbs.
Some investigators believe these orbs are spirit energy.
Video cameras can capture unexplained happenings,
such as doors slamming.

A GHOST-HUNTING PAL

The BooBuddy is a ghost-hunting teddy bear. Investigators can leave the bear in an area they believe is haunted. The bear tracks temperature and EMF changes. It also records EVP on its own!

thermal camera

OK

Thermal cameras help investigators pick up on unusually warm and cold objects in a room. These signal a possible ghostly presence. Some people believe colder areas mean a ghost is trying to appear. **Ambient thermometers** also track these sudden temperature changes.

EERIE EXPLANATIONS

Almost half of Americans believe in ghosts. Still, **skeptics** question their existence. They believe there are simpler explanations for evidence. Orbs in photos may result from dust. Cold spots could come from leaky windows.

Evidence can be faked as well. People have confessed to tricking others into believing paranormal events. The famous Maggie Fox once said she and her sister had faked their ghostly talents. Experts have proven many ghost photos and recordings as fake.

SLEEP PARALYSIS

Many claims of ghost encounters may be explained by sleep paralysis. During sleep paralysis, a person wakes up but cannot move. In this state, they may see things that are not really there!

Ghost-hunting gadgets do not sway skeptics either.
EMF meters can be affected by common devices like cell
phones. Static and background noises on EVP recordings
can make "messages" unclear. Investigators may hear
what they want to hear.

PARANORMAL PODS

Sometimes investigators use devices called REM Pods. These release their own EMF. Colorful lights signal when fields from possible ghosts interrupt their own.

Skeptics claim that ghost hunting is a **pseudoscience**. There is no proof that ghosts exist. So how can investigators know that EMF meters, thermometers, and other devices will detect a ghost's presence? Using scientific tools does not necessarily make an investigation scientific.

THE SEARCH FOR PROOF

Investigators have studied ghosts for years. There are more than 3,000 ghost-hunting groups in the United States alone. Yet no investigation has unearthed solid proof of ghosts.

Even so, many investigators trust that ghosts exist. Some think current technology is not advanced enough to find ghosts. Others believe ghost hunting needs to return to the basics. Fancy new gadgets are not the key. Instead, research methods must depend on **hypotheses** and observation. Either way, until proof comes, ghosts will remain a mystery.

GHOSTS TO GO

The Traveling Museum of the Paranormal and the
Occult brings haunted objects from city to city.
The collection includes a haunted radio. The radio
can turn itself on and tune to channels that play
whispering voices!

GLOSSARY

afterlife—the place where people's souls may go after death

ambient thermometers—devices that measure the temperature of the surrounding air

audio recordings—sounds captured and saved by a device called an audio recorder

Civil War—the U.S. war between the Union, or northern states, and the Confederacy, or southern states, fought between 1861 and 1865

electromagnetic field (EMF)—a force caused by the movement of electricity that creates magnetic energy

electronic voice phenomena (EVP)—strange sounds on electronic recordings believed to be spirit voices

evidence—information that helps prove or disprove something

hypotheses—educated guesses that form the basis of an investigation

investigators—people who try to find out the facts about something in order to learn if or how it happened

mainstream—the ideas considered normal by the most people

mediums—people who claim they can communicate with spirits

paranormal—unable to be explained using science

pseudoscience—a collection of methods incorrectly believed to be scientific

psychical—psychic; psychic people have powers of the mind that cannot be explained by science.

séances—gatherings where people try to communicate with spirits

skeptics—people who doubt something is true

souls—the spiritual part of humans; some believe the soul gives life to a person's body.

Spiritualism—a religion that believes ghosts can communicate with living people

static—noise from a radio or television, often caused by electricity

thermal cameras—cameras that can pick up on and show heat

TO LEARN MORE

AT THE LIBRARY

Reed, Ellis M. *Ghost Hunting*. Mankato, Minn.: Capstone Press, 2018.

Richard, Orlin. *Ghosts*. Mankato, Minn.: Child's World, 2015.

Winters, Jaime. *Haunted at Sea*. New York, N.Y.: Crabtree Publishing Company, 2018.

ON THE WEB

Learning more about ghosts is as easy as 1, 2, 3.

1. Go to www.factsurfer.com.

2. Enter "ghosts" into the search box.

3. Click the "Surf" button and you will see a list of related web sites.

With factsurfer.com, finding more information is just a click away.

INDEX

The images in this book are reproduced through the courtesy of: Fresnel, front cover (woman); Joe Prachatree, front cover (ghost), p. 23 (ghost); vitalez, front cover; Yuriy Seleznev, pp. 2-3; ehrlif, pp. 4-5; Rawpixel, p. 5; Antlio, p. 6 (ghost); movieprop, pp. 6-7; Gullatawat Putchagarn, pp. 8-9; The Picture Art Collection/ Alamy, p. 10 (left); Hulton Deutsch/ Getty, p. 10 (right); Renphoto, pp. 10-11; William H. Mumler/ John Paul Getty Museum, p. 12 (insets); Library of Congress/Corbis/VCG/ Getty, pp. 12-13; SFIO CRACHO, pp. 14-15; Guy Solimano/Syfy/ NBCU Photo Bank/ Getty Images, p. 15 (inset); super101, p. 16 (inset); Chris Underwood, p. 17 (top); Peter Underwood/ Mary Evans Picture Library, p. 17 (bottom); Jacek Rogoz, pp. 18-19; Syda Productions, pp. 20-21; spectrefloat/ Flickr, p. 22 (inset); Gergely Zsolnai, pp. 22-23; Evgeniia Trushkova, p. 23 (thermal camera); Netfalls Remy Musser, pp. 24-25; Vince Talotta, pp. 26-27; Jandrie Lombard, pp. 28-29 (people); phoelixDE, pp. 28-29; ARTFULLY PHOTOGRAPHER, p. 29 (ghost).